Like everything that is ... ible without the unconditional love, ... s support of my lovely bride, Kathryn. Every day she teaches me that the impossible things are the only things worth doing. Thank you my dear. Forever is where it begins.

My three sons, Eric, Edward, and Alexander have also offered support and encouragement simply by being the men they are. The way they each live their lives serve as constant reminders to me that play and work can be the same thing. Each of them is a hero of mine.

I also need to thank my dear friend Frank Coster. It was an email from Frank, in the fall of 2003, that set me on the path to learn about, and instantly fall in love with, the great game of Cricket.

As long as I'm thanking Franks, I need to also thank Frank Pichen who has always been my go-to guy on all things Baseball. In fact, Frank was a huge help when I wrote my first Cricket/Baseball article for the Bradman Boundary Magazine.

Many other thanks go to all the Cricket lovers that I have met around the World, in boardrooms, in pubs, in taxis, at seminars, on exhibit floors, and anyplace else that I seized a chance to talk about Cricket. Thank you, one and all, for sharing your passion with me. A special thanks here to Jim Patel for all the Cricket tapes and talks over the counter at the gas station.

Of course, no Cricket book from me would be complete without a shout-out to the Monkey Butlers the world round. The Monkey Butlers are an international body of true Cricket nutters. We formed as a group in the spring of 2004 and we remain strongly united today. You lot know who you are and you should be proud that one of our number actually got a book written, let alone published!

One more special thank you goes to my friend Michael Ball in Australia. Michael has been a great mentor on my path to learning and loving Cricket. Michael welcomed me into his country, into his farm, into my association with the Bradman Museum and the International Cricket Hall of Fame, and also into the SCG's member's bar! Michael, I hope you know the impact you have had on me. This small mention does not begin to repay the debt of gratitude I owe you.

The book you see on your screen, or hold in your hand, would simply not be possible without the incredible help of my buddy Myron and his amazing team. No way this book happens without them.

It would be ridiculous for me to thank anybody for anything and not include my parents. My father, Big Ed Johnson, has been a sportsman and sports fan his whole life. While not a fan of Cricket per se, he does appreciate all sport and he certainly loves America and freedom!

Sadly, my mother did not live to see this book published. However, her memory, love, and support are always with me. She raised seven sporting children who have dozens of championships among them. She was, perhaps, the kindest and most loving person to have ever walked this earth.

LOOK MA, I WROTE A BOOK!

Takoma Ridge Media

Five Reasons Why Cricket is More American than Baseball

Published in the United States of America.

eBook ISBN 978-0-9836382-2-3

Print ISBN 978-0-9836382-3-0

First Edition: July 2011

TABLE OF CONTENTS

SECTION ONE

Just a few things to get you ready for the good stuff

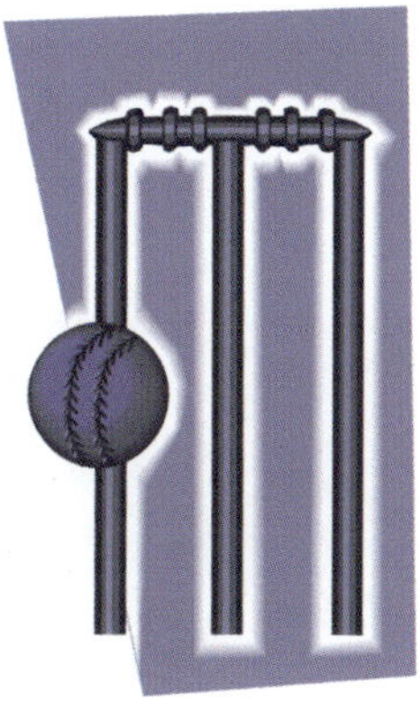

Apologies

As a cradle Catholic, I learned very early in life that just about everything that happens is my fault and that I should apologize for it and repent. Therefore, I would like to begin this book with a series of apologizes so that those apologizes do not litter up the interesting parts.

I would like to apologize for anything in this book that might offend or confuse the reader. I wrote this book with a blend of passion for Cricket and a desire to inform my fellow Americans about the great game. No doubt, in my effort to inform, I have written a few things that may offend those who can't look past the style of my writing. For those offenses I am deeply sorry.

I would like to apologize for using American English spellings and sayings since all the other parts of the Cricketing world use some form of the Queen's English. There are two reasons for my choice. First, the President of Merriam-Webster, John Morse, is a friend of mine and I always try to honor that friendship by using "his" English. In this case, it is doubly important since John went to Haverford College which is the only college in America to have a Varsity Cricket team. Second, while there will no doubt be a massive world-wide audience for this book, the primary purpose is to explain all of this to my fellow Americans. The topic is complex enough. Asking the readers to follow along and keep up while having to simultaneously translate English-to-English is simply too much to ask. After all, I'm trying to help people. Here again, I am deeply sorry.

I would like to apologize to anyone who is a Cricket or Baseball purest. I am one hundred percent confident that I have misstated/overstated some aspect or another about the games in question. Please understand that this small book is intended to be a comparison of freedoms, or lack thereof, within the games and not a detailed analysis of either. I am making no attempt to explain the deep nuances or subtleties of either game. For those of you who would take me to task for not getting minute details right in either or both sports, I apologize.

Last, but in no way least, I would like to apologize to my legion of female readers. Throughout this book I use the phrases *he, him, and his* to represent the players of both games. Women play Cricket too and they are very good at. It is simply a lack of will to fight with my editor that caused me to take the easy way out, rather than use he/she, etc. Ladies, please forgive me.

As Sister Mary Hitsalot taught us all to say back at Our Lady of Perpetual Torment,

Mea culpa
Mea culpa
Mea maxima culpa.

A Bit of Background

In order to help you, dear reader, understand why Cricket is more American than Baseball, it is important that I offer you a bit of an introduction to Cricket. The great game itself has been explained countless times in countless books by many authors who are far more qualified than I on the history and complexities of Cricket. Among those countless books are many true gems. My favorites are 1) *What Is a Googly? The Mysteries of Cricket Explained*, by Rob Eastaway 2) *Tom Smith's Cricket Umpiring and Scoring*, by Tom Smith and 3) *Wisden's The Laws of Cricket*, by Don Oslear.

I will not insult the authors of those fine works by attempting to offer a detailed treatment of the great game. Rather, I will offer, for your kind consideration, a few key concepts that are shared between Baseball and Cricket and a few key concepts that are different. In order to provide a bit more detail, a modest glossary of some terms, both similar and different, appears toward the end of this book.

Baseball and Cricket have a great deal in common. Both games are played primarily in summer weather (keeping in mind summer comes at different times around the world). Both games are intended to be played on natural grass and outdoors. Both games have a player with a bat who generally attempts to hit a thrown ball. Both games have players in the field who attempt to catch the ball and/or get the ball into a specific location before the runner gets there.

Both games have a certain segment of their fan-bases who are totally obsessed with extremely detailed statistics. Finally, both games are viewed by many fans as a lovely way to waste an afternoon, have a few drinks, perhaps catch a nap, and enjoy the sunshine.

Now that you have learned (you were paying attention, right?) a bit about the similarities, perhaps I should point out a few of the differences.

In Baseball there are nine innings and in Cricket there are up to, but not always, two. In Cricket there are up to ten outs per inning and in Baseball there are three. There is no limit to the amount of times a batter/batsman can bat in a Baseball game and in Cricket the maximum is two.

In Cricket there are eleven players and in Baseball there are nine. Baseball allows for a wide variety of substitutions. In fact, some players are specifically tasked to be substitutes such as relief pitchers and pinch hitters. However, a Baseball player who has been substituted for may not return. In Cricket, substitutions are frowned upon and are often only temporary while a player tends to certain physical needs. Next time you see me, ask about a certain Ricky Ponting story from an England/Australia Test Match back in 2005.

In Baseball, arguing with umpire (often loudly and lewdly) is considered part of the game and is only punishable in extreme cases. In Cricket the umpire's word is absolute and any complaint, beyond the simplest of mutterings, can lead to very negative consequences such as losing your pay for that match.

In Cricket, the ball is replaced only at specific intervals or when the ball is very severely deformed. In Baseball, the ball is replaced with alarming regularity and at the seeming whim of both player and umpire. In fact, Major League Baseball requires the home side to have at least 90 balls on hand before the game begins.

In Baseball, there is only one format for playing a professional game. That format being alternative sides batting for nine innings, with the minor variance of the home team does not bat in the last half of the ninth inning if they are already ahead. If the teams are tied at the end of nine innings, the game will continue until either the home team is ahead after the visiting team finishes any extra inning or the home team finishes their extra inning and the visiting team is ahead. In fact, there is no specific rule in Baseball that ends a game if the score is tied. In theory a Baseball game can continue until the end of time.

In modern day international Cricket, there are three main forms of the game. Test Cricket, which is the traditional long form that can take up to five days to play. One Day International (ODI), which takes a full day to play. Twenty20, which takes about three hours. Regardless of the form of the game, at the end of scheduled play, the game is over even if the score is tied. In days gone by, there were truly wonderful things called "Timeless Tests" that were played until both innings were completed. Here again, when next you see me ask about the Test match in Durban during the 1930s.

A Few Other Items for Your Consideration

Although virtually unknown in the United States, Cricket is the second most popular sport in the world, behind what Americans call soccer but what most of the rest of the world calls football. That little wording problem may well lead to another book.

As you sit there and wonder,"How could Cricket be the world's second most popular sport when we Americans know so little about it?", consider the following fact. The world's second, sixth, and eight most heavily populated countries are totally mad about Cricket.

In India, Pakistan, and Bangladesh,Cricket has a place as almost a national religion. When key Cricket matches are being played these countries grind to almost a complete stop. Imagine the SuperBowl going on for five days. Then imagine there are none of those annoying people who say that they don't like sports. Then multiple that by about 100. You are starting to get the idea.

Military hostilities have even been suspended so that Cricket matches can be played and enjoyed in peace. When I say mad about Cricket, I really mean mad about Cricket.

It is also important to point out that the United States has a very nice Cricket history, even if we haven't been paying much attention for the last 100 years or so. The first ever international Cricket match was played by the United States and Canada, or more precisely "The British Empire's Canadian Province", way back in 1844. The New York based match, played over three days, was watched by almost 20,000 people. Those people are rumored to have placed over $120,000 worth of wagers. Sadly, the US fell to the Canadians by 23 runs. A follow up match was played in Canada in 1845 with the Canadians once again winning. Over the past 165 years things have gone continually downhill for cricket in the USA.

Perhaps more important to point out is that there is a vibrant and growing Cricket movement in the United States. We have a national governing body, The United States of America Cricket Association (USACA), and a series of leagues and teams that spans from sea to shining sea.

There are cricket tournaments and festivals all over America. Perhaps the most important and interesting of those festivals is the Philadelphia International Cricket Festival. Each spring, dedicated folks from the greater Philadelphia area put on a wonderful tournament that features players from all around the world. You can find out more about this great event at www.cricketfestival.com

Wait, I Thought You Were an American

Since my great and glorious Cricket journey began, virtually every time I start talking to a new person who knows something about Cricket the same thing happens. The conversation goes along very well for the first minute or two and then my conversational partner stops and says something along the lines of "Wait, I thought you were an American".

When this happens, as it inevitably does, I smile and say something like "Yes, I am an American. Could we get back to the Cricket talk please?" This back-and-forth goes on for a few minutes with questions like "Are your parents English (Aussies, Kiwis, South Africans)?" or "Have you spent time living abroad?". Once or twice "Did you marry a (Insert member of a Commonwealth Nation here)?" Nope, sorry to disappoint. I'm just a regular American. I think I have fielded more questions about my "real" birthplace than President Obama.

I'd like to set the record straight and clear once and for all. I was born and raised in and around our Nation's Capital, Washington D.C., as were all six of my siblings. Both my parents were also born and raised in Washington. Throughout my parents lives and down through the lives of we seven children, my family has witnessed, up close and personal, just about everything important that has happened in this country in the 20th and 21st Centuries, both good and bad, right in "our neighborhood". Suffice it to say, that I am really a 100% American!

Once the questions of my birthplace, my heritage, and the places where I have lived (all in the USA) have been settled, the next question is almost always "How did you get involved in Cricket?".

As is indicated on the Many Thanks page, Frank Coster is the man responsible for introducing me to Cricket. Frank lives now in America's neighbor to the North (a.k.a. Canada), but he is originally from a small town in the south of England near Brighton. During the autumn of 2003, Frank sent me an email that went something like this --- "England are coming to the West Indies in the spring. Do you fancy a week in Barbados to watch the Cricket?".

My initial reaction was negative. This had nothing to do with Frank or with Cricket. It had to do with the location. You see, Barbados has lots and lots of three things I really don't like. Those things are Sun, Sand, and Water. I realize that almost all Americans would jump at a chance to spend an early April week on a Caribbean island. Me, not so much.

After a great talk with my amazing wife, Frank's idea started to take on a shine of promise. Kathryn pointed out that I had been working way too hard for way too long and that I haven't had time away without any responsibility in ages. Kathryn also reminded me that I always enjoy time with Frank. In this very important way, Kathryn became a key person on my journey to Cricket madness.

A quick talk with my boss at the time, Ross Follett, to ensure all was also clear work-wise, and then all systems were go for my first Cricket trip. Simple and quick as that. The whole thing happened in about two days. There was another quick flurry of logistics (plane trip, hotel, Cricket tickets, etc.) and then all I had to do was to wait for Spring.

During the intervening months, my friend Jim Patel starting giving me tips on Cricket and even lent me tapes of Cricket matches that he recorded off the satellite. Jim is from Gujarat State in India and like his billion plus countrymen, he is VERY into Cricket.

Frank sent along some books. I watched some Cricket live on DirecTV and off of some DVDs. The winter set in, and we have a lot of winter in Wisconsin, and I grew more excited about the trip.

The trip itself was fantastic! Frank and I deftly managed to avoid the Sun (watching Cricket all day from seats under cover), the Sand (never got closer to the beach than a rum shack across the street), and the Water (beyond showers, not a drop).

On the plane trip from Miami to Barbados, I met Alex and Brian. Alex is from England and Brian from New Zealand. They were my row-mates on the flight and they were fighting like those two old guys from the Muppet show. Once they started to believe that I was really going to Barbados for the Cricket (see earlier portion of this section), they assured me we would see each other at the Test. Being used to major sporting events having crowds of more than 80,000 people, I wasn't so sure about that.

Cricket in Barbados is a much more manageable affair than any major American sport. Sure enough, I was headed back to my seat after a beer run on the second day, and there were Alex and Brian. We had surely bonded and we remain close to this day. In fact, we just had beers (several actually) in London this past April as part of a mini Monkey Butler reunion. By way of completeness, I should add in a mention of Bill and his blue trumpet, the wheelbarrow, Gareth, Roger, Rob, James, and a few assorted Barmy Army members who came to the match dressed as Nuns, Popes, Catholic School Girls, Apes, or many other, shall we say, interesting get-ups. All of these encounters happened during my first trip to Barbados.

The Cricket was super fantastic! England won in Barbados for the first time since 1968 and that was the first English team ever to win three Test Matches in the same Caribbean trip. Matthew Hoggard got a hat-trick (don't worry about what that means), Graham Thorpe got a ton (don't worry about that either), and a young England up-and-comer named Freddie Flintoff was starting to show the depth of his greatness by taking 7 wickets in a single Test, with 5 of those wickets coming in one inning.

After the match was over, in a brief three days I might add, we (and I mean all 16,000 in attendance) were having a great time in a pub in St. Lawerence Gap, which is a particularly English section of the island. While we were all going over what seemed like every run and out of the entire match, in walked 8 members of England's team.

That's right; almost the entire English team just walked in the pub where we were celebrating. Can you imagine most of the starting lineup of the Yankees or the Giants coming into a local bar after having won an important Baseball series? It was a truly amazing experience, and it was at that moment, that I began to form a real love for this great game. The players were kind, easy to get along with, and happy to chat. Yes, you guessed it, as I met each of them, they said something along the lines of "Wait, I thought you were an American". During that amazing evening, I meet several of England's team. The most incredible part, was a lovely chat I had, punctuated with more than one pint, with Freddie Flintoff.

When I got up the next morning, I knew I was 100% hooked for life on Cricket.

Michael Johnson having pints with Freddie Flintoff in Barbados

Freedom

If you read the last chapter, and shame on you if you didn't, you now know that I am a 100% American. Like every other American, and the millions of people from around the world who strive to become Americans, I was raised to believe the central truth that America is all about FREEDOM.

Understandably, we Americans are very proud of our freedoms and all the benefits they convey. We have fought, and continue to fight, many wars to build this nation and to protect the freedoms we hold so dear.

Freedom of Religion, Freedom of Assembly, Freedom of Speech, are key aspects of what America is all about and what it means to be an American. These are the core tenets of the U.S. Constitution, The Bill of Rights, and all the subsequent amendments and legislation that govern our fair land.

Apparently, these freedoms do not convey into the world of sport and certainly not to the game of Baseball.

Alas, I must report to you that Baseball, the game that likes to refer to itself as America's Past-time, is actually a game that restricts the players' freedom so tightly it might well have been invented by Uncle Joe Stalin. Truth be told, there is very little freedom in the game at all.

Cricket, on the other hand, is a game that allows a tremendous amount of freedom for its players even within a set of regulations referred to as the Laws of Cricket. Yes, our one-time oppressor, the United Kingdom, has developed a game that more truly represents the American way than anything the USA has to offer.

These are not matters of opinion, but rather matters of fact. The game of Baseball is so riddled with constrictions it is a minor miracle that the game can played and enjoyed at all. Little wonder that Baseball continues to slip farther and farther from the nation's consciousness. Having been long ago replaced by Football as America's number one sport, Baseball continues to restrict the freedom of the game and its spectators with each new rule and regulation.

It is only fair for me to admit that I was never much a Baseball fan. This has pretty much always been true but become 100% true when I was a young man when greed and avarice struck the second time and the Washington Senators once again abandoned DC. That time, in 1971, to become the Texas Rangers. The first time was when they left to become the Minnesota Twins.

However, the undoing of the game itself can hardly be blamed on me. This book intends to explain that by constantly restricting both the players and the fans of Baseball with a suffocating pile of rules and regulations, the game itself loudly proclaims just how un-American it is.

Make no mistake, I love my country. I just don't care much for a game that is so bent on restricting freedoms. I close this chapter with a single word that should make my position on the matter very clear.

AMERICA!

SECTION TWO
FREEDOM

CHAPTER ONE

Freedom One

Who Decides Whether a Ball Is Good or Bad?

For the sake of purity, I will refer to the action of sending the ball to the batter as being *pitched* in the Baseball setting and *bowled* in the Cricket setting.

Baseball

In the heavily oppressive game that is Baseball, the batter has a constant and menacing presence called the Home Plate Umpire. This dark and looming force decides, seemingly on a whim, whether each pitched ball is a good one (a "strike") or a bad one (a "ball"). If the batter chooses, in this supposed land of choice, to allow the pitched balls to pass him by, he is at risk of being dismissed if the Home Plate Umpire determines three of those balls were strikes. When this occurs, the batter is simply called OUT and set back to the bench.

This menacing condition is equally bad for the pitcher. If the Home Plate Umpire decides four of those pitches are balls, then the batter is allowed to advance to first base without having done a thing. Here again, the decision of ball or strike is done seemingly on a whim.

Baseball's rules do indicate some particulars as to what is to be called a ball and what is to be called a strike. However, the application of these particulars is done is such a haphazard fashion as to render the rules worthless and to restrict the freedom of the batter and the pitcher almost to the point of supplication to the umpire.

If you doubt this premise in any way, all you need do is watch two Baseball games and try to guess which pitch is a ball or a strike. There is no doubt that no human alive could successfully do so with any level of consistency.

In this fundamental way, by restricting freedom on the very element that begins each play, Baseball proves itself to be a game that strips both the batter and the pitcher of the most basic right of freedom to practice their respective crafts.

Cricket

In the liberating game that is Cricket, the batsman has complete control of what balls to play and which ones to let pass. Yes, there is a hazard to letting a bowled ball go without contact as it could knock over the stumps and the batter would be dismissed. Unlike in Baseball, there is no whim or fancy here. If the stumps are not struck and the bails do not fall, there is no other party who decides if the batter is out. Regardless of the hazard, the batsman retains the freedom to swing, hit, or let pass whichever balls he chooses. In any case, except when the ball would hit the stumps, the batsman can (and often does) let lots of balls go by with nothing more than mild interest.

The batsman may also make swings and misses on as many balls as he pleases as long as the ball doesn't hit the stumps. There is nobody to force him to do anything but himself. If he doesn't contact the ball and the ball doesn't hit the stumps, nobody will decide he is dismissed and send him off the field. Nor will anyone decide he has had too many bad balls and send him off to the next spot and bring on another batsman.

Many a batsman has batted well by batting sparingly. Just do a little research on the maddeningly slow play of Geoffery Boycott if you want to learn how much effort can be put into accomplishing nothing while batting. Many other batsmen have swung wildly and often, sometimes even switching sides during the bowling delivery (TALK ABOUT FREEDOM!) in an effort to play a particular kind of shot.

For the bowler, there is no pressure to hit an exact and specific place to get the batsman out. While there is an umpire who looks, very closely I might add, on how the ball is bowled and where it goes once it is bowled, he doesn't interfere with the bowler's or the batsman's choices.

The Laws are very complex, but they are also very clear as to what is allowed or disallowed. What the Laws don't do is place the freedom of where to bowl and how to bat in the hands of the umpire.

Like the batsman, many a bowler has bowled very well by hitting a specific line and length without being awarded anything for the effort. Rather than some cheap and immediate reward from an umpire, the bowler patiently works a spot in a cat and mouse game with the batsman that pits the two against each other and not an official.

There are also bowlers, spinners mostly, who bowl the ball way "outside" only to have it snap back into the stumps and catch the batter off his guard. To watch a spinner blow up the stumps of a batsman is one of the most amazing things in sport. Even after seeing the replay again and again, one is forced to remain in absolute bewilderment as how the bowler made it happen.

As with Baseball there are significant restrictions on where the bowler can be when he releases the ball. However, Cricket only restricts the end of the delivery, not the entire motion. In Baseball, the pitcher is restricted to a two foot long by six inch wide strip of rubber from which he must pitch the ball. The pitcher must remain in contact with the rubber until he is prepared to release the ball. He may only move towards the batter from a standstill. If he breaks contact with the rubber at any point in his delivery, that pitch is invalid (called a Balk), the pitch is ruled a Ball, and any runners at the other bases are allowed to advance one base.

In Cricket; where the bowler starts his approach is left totally up to him. The spinners will typically take several rather slow-motion steps before they release the ball. Their's is not a craft of speed, but of movement. They rely on the action of the ball to confuse and confound the batsman rather than trying to blow the ball past him. A spinner is a rough analog to Baseball knuckleballer. The spinner's ball does some odd things while it is in the air and when it hits the ground it can do unimaginable things. "Hits the ground?" you are probably saying. Sorry, did I leave that bit out before? Yes, in Cricket the bowled ball almost always hits the ground before it reaches the batsman.

The fast-bowlers, however, may well build up a great head of steam by sprinting in from twenty yards or more before they release the ball. Their attack, as the name would imply, is all about speed. They get a huge run up as they come towards the batsman and then they unleash the ball at 90-100MPH. When it hits the ground, it can be a truly dangerous thing as the Cricket ball is smaller and harder than a Baseball and it tends to go all sorts of places. Many of those places involve contact with the batsman's body. Unlike in Baseball, a hit batsman receives no reward for being hit beyond perhaps a nice ball-mark or a broken bone. There is a possible bonus. If the ball hits the batsman and gets past the fielders, runs can be scored on a "leg-bye".

The batsman may not block the wicket with his body. If the ball is on a trajectory to strike the wicket and it hits the batsman's body, he is out "Leg before Wicket". The basic idea is that you have a large bat in your hands and you must use it and not your body to protect the wicket.

Final word!

The bottom line on this comparison is that the Baseball batter and pitcher are each so heavily restricted by the umpires and their irregular application of the restrictive rules of the game, as to choke out almost all the freedom that should be afforded in an American game. Meanwhile, Cricket has created an environment within which each individual has tremendous control about how they perform their duties on each and every play of the game.

Freedom Score	Cricket	1
	Baseball	0

CHAPTER TWO

Freedom Two

What Happens When the Batter Does Hit the Ball?

Now that it has been clearly established that the two most fundamental actions in Baseball, pitching and batting, are both so lacking in freedom that they might actually qualify as punishment, we can move on to what is allowed to go on in the event that bat does strike ball.

Sadly, the previous chapter is only the beginning of how badly Baseball limits freedoms. If you thought there was trouble in Chapter 1, wait until you read about this mess.

Once again, virtually all freedom and creativity has been stripped from the Baseball player while the Cricketer enjoys limitless freedom in the area of batting. The Baseball trouble begins before the ball is even pitched. In Baseball the batter is restricted to a very modest area, called the batter's box, which is only four feet by six feet, from which he is forced to practice his craft. If the batter steps outside that box and hits the ball he is automatically out no matter where the ball goes. A pretty sorry start for the poor batter, you must admit.

If the Baseball batter manages to overcome the restricted freedoms from Chapter 1 and the additional restriction of the batter's box, he must now avoid an even larger menace, The Foul Line. While the outfield dimensions of a Baseball field allow for some pretty serious freedom, on the part of the field designers and not the players, there is no avoiding The Foul Line. The Foul line tells us what batted balls are "fair" and might allow the batter to advance and which are "foul" and therefore will not allow the batter a chance to advance. The Foul line starts at Home Plate and forms the perimeter of a 90 degree area called Fair Territory. The line extends all the way to the fenced boundary. In essence, this chalky white menace crushes most of the batter's freedom by only allowing him to safely hit the ball within that 90 degree area. The remaining 270 degrees represent Foul Territory and are therefore not allowed to be used for the batter to safely advance.

As is illustrated below, The Foul Line is omnipresent and very oppressive.

By contrast, the Cricket Batsman enjoys 100% freedom on where he may hit the ball. That's right 100% freedom. There is no batter's box to constrain his movements. He can move about as he sees fit in order to best position himself to swing (if he wishes to) at the incoming ball. When the Cricket Batsman chooses to exercise his freedom to swing at whichever ball he wishes (Freedom 1), he may hit the ball the full 360 degrees. As the picture below shows, there is no looming specter of a Foul Line to oppress the batter into only hitting the ball certain places. The boundary rope in Cricket exists as a scoring mechanism (see 4s and 6s) and not as a vehicle to limit the batsman's freedom.

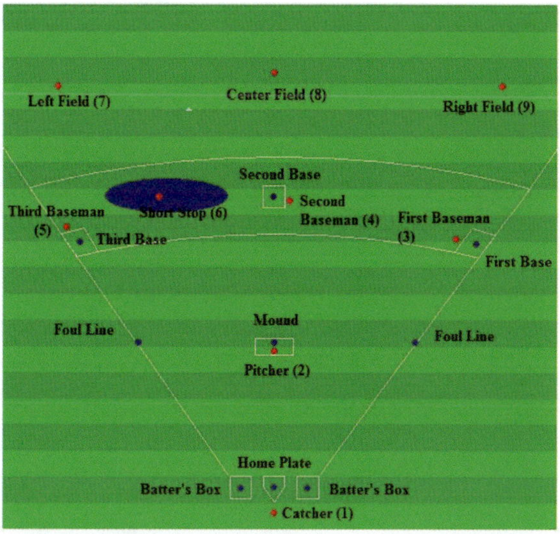

All Bases are 90' Apart
Mound is 60'6" from Home Plate
Numbers Denote Positions for Score Book Purposes

Baseball Diamond

Cricket: Fielding positions for a right-handed batsman

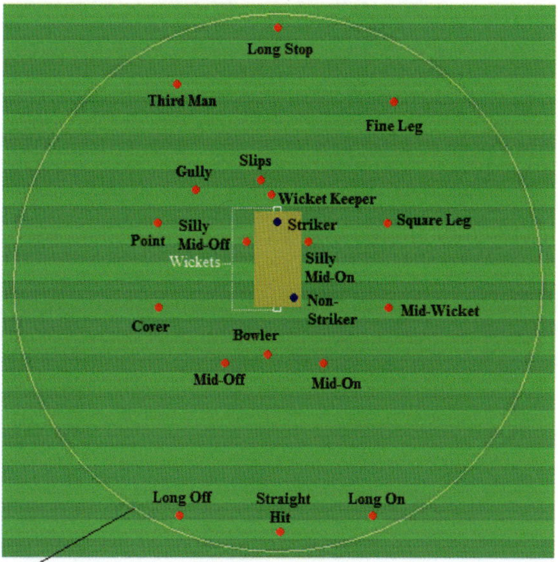

Boundary Rope

There are 66 feet between wickets

Cricket Field

In Cricket there are no draconian restrictions on the batsman's choice of where to play the ball. He may literally hit it anywhere he chooses. Let me type that again. He may literally hit is anywhere he chooses. That's right, all 360 degrees. Yes, I mean anywhere and everywhere. Yes, that does include behind him! Any more questions?

Admittedly, in Cricket, the opposing side does have two more players in the field than a Baseball team who are trying to get the batter out. However, the fielding side must cover EVERYWHERE with their fielders. If one does the rather simple math, you will find that the amount of territory each Cricketer must cover is 32+ degrees while a Baseball player is only asked to cover 10 degrees. Taking that simple math just one step further, you would find that a Baseball team would only be allowed three fielders if they were required to cover an equal amount of field. It actually boggles the mind to consider how much a Cricketer must do while he is just "standing around in the sun".

There is an additional freedom in Cricket with regard to the field itself. The groundskeeper is allowed to grow just about anything he likes within the field of play. A nice reference point would be the Saint Lawrence ground in Canterbury, where for a long time Kent played their matches with a tree growing in the outfield.

A Final Sad Note on this Topic

It brings me no pleasure to remind my fellow Americans that the Foul Line has an even darker side to it. If the oppressed Baseball batter defies the tyranny of the Foul Lines, he can still be caught out in Foul Territory without any hope of him being able to advance. Take a minute and think about that. His freedom has already been severely restricted by way of controlling the location where he can safely hit the ball and now he has the added negative bonus of possibly being caught out. Could things be any less American than that? Who thinks up these things, Fidel Castro? Oh, wait a minute. The Cubans are really good at Baseball. Sets the mind to wondering, doesn't it?

ADVANTAGE CRICKET

Freedom Score	Cricket	2
	Baseball	0

CHAPTER THREE

Freedom Three

OK, So What about the Running?

Baseball

It is difficult to come up with a more vivid image to describe The American Way than to say one is Running Free. In fact, one of America's greatest singer/songwriters, Bruce Springsteen, had a massive rock-n-roll hit with *Born to Run* because the song so touched the meaning of what it means to be an American.

It is, therefore, all the more tragic when one realizes the virtually paralyzing restrictions that are placed on running and runners in Baseball. Yes, even in that most obviously freeing aspect of Baseball, freedom is almost absent. It is the sad, sad truth.

These restrictions start at the first part of a Batter's turn and are also present at the end. Let's begin at the beginning. If a batter does manage the minor miracle of overcoming the restrictions of Freedom #1 and #2, and puts the ball into play by hitting it in Fair Territory, he must immediately run to first base. While this is not an arduous journey since it is only 90 feet, it is perilous since there are several fielders within very close proximity. It is important to add that all these fielders wear gloves or mitts and can easily field the hardest hit balls. The batter has no other course of action even if he only hits the ball two feet. He must run or he will undoubtedly be thrown out before he gets to first base. The only other approach, which is often taken, is to just surrender and be out at first base anyway.

In some way, even this fate is better than having no chance at all. Of course, we all remember the end of the last chapter where the batter can be caught out with no options at all.

Now let's move on to the end of the batter's time at bat. Even when he accomplishes all that is asked of him and hits a Home Run (roughly equivalent to a '6' in Cricket), he still must stop batting. While not technically out, he is restricted from batting again until all of his teammates complete their turn at bat. Yes, you understand this correctly. The Baseball batter can do all within his power and can accomplish the highest possible positive outcome and his reward is to be stripped of the opportunity to continue batting. Even when he hits a thundering Home Run that might leave the stadium entirely, his turn at bat is over. Here again, there is an added negative bonus. When the Baseball batter hits a Home Run, he is still required to run, mostly just jog, around all four bases before he is credited with his reward. This is true even though the fielding team cannot possibly get him out. Actually, this aspect of Baseball even gets one step worse. If the Batsman does not complete this rounding of the bases to the Umpire's satisfaction, he can be called out and he will not be credited with his runs. Utter madness!

There is another freedom limiting aspect of running the bases in Baseball. Even when the runner manages to make it safely to the next base, he may not run past the base without risking being run out. That's right, the runner can safely reach a base, but he must stay in contact with that base or else he might get out. Oddly, this is 100% true of 2nd and 3rd base. This quirk is partially true of 1st base (the runner may continue only if he stays in foul territory) and not relevant at all at Home Plate since the batter/runner is finished for that time at bat anyway.

Cricket

In the wide open and freedom loving game of Cricket, these restrictions, or any others that would be in any way similar,are nowhere to be found. If the Cricket batsman exercises his freedom of choice to swing at a ball (Freedom 1) and then hits it anywhere he likes (Freedom 2), he needn't run if he doesn't wish to.

Yes, yes, I know that accumulating runs is an important part of batting. I also know that freedom to **not run** or not even attempt to do so in central to the batting ethos of Cricket.

Just to make sure everyone understands this, I'll state it even more directly. There is nothing in the Laws of Cricket that compels the batsman to run, EVER! While it is considered bad form to bat too long without putting in some running effort, this occurs so rarely that most fans have never seen it.

Therefore, if a Cricket batsman hits a little nurdler a few feet away from his bat, he does not need to make the same mad and futile dash to the next spot that a Baseball batter must. This particular aspect of Cricket is a grand thing as it not only saves the embarrassment for the batsman who has hit this weak ball, but it also prevents the fans from being deprived of watching that batsman have a great day batting.

Now it is only fair to point out that Cricket does require both batsmen (striker and non-striker) to safely switch ends in order to score a run. However, this just another wonderful aspect of the game and not a restriction of the batsman's freedom of choice when it comes to running. OK, that's all settled. The beginning of a batsman's turn at bat, in fact every ball in a batsman's turn at bat, comes with a 100% freedom to run if the batsman wishes.

On we go to the business of continuing to bat. In Cricket, the batsman is allowed to bat until the other side gets him out. This could be on the first ball. This could also, theoretically, last for every ball of the full allotment of five days. There is simply nothing in the Laws that forces a batsman to stop batting unless he is out. Like Baseball, there are many ways for a batsman to get out. Unlike Baseball, hitting the best possible shot for the highest possible one ball result is not one of them.

Cricket has a conceptual analog to the Baseball Home Run. When a Cricket batsman hits the ball beyond the boundary rope (more on that later) without the ball hitting the ground, it is referred to as a '6'. Very simply, this is because the batsman is awarded six runs for this bit of batting excellence. However, Cricket does not punish the batsman by forcing him to stop batting. In fact, Cricket doesn't even make the batsman run back and forth six times in order to collect the runs. He has accomplished the task, he gets his reward. Once the Umpire sees the ball clear the boundary, he raises both arms (not unlike an American Football Referee signaling a Touchdown) and the running stops and the batsman gets his runs.

Cricket also has a conceptual analog to the Baseball Ground Rule Double. When a Cricket batsman hits the ball beyond the boundary rope on a least one bounce, it is ruled a '4'. Here again, this is because the batsman is awarded four runs for this act of batting skill. Once the umpire sees the ball cross the boundary rope, he moves his arm in front of him in a motion somewhat like a small ocean wave. The running stops and the batsman still gets his runs.

In both cases, the batsman merely returns to his spot and continues batting. There is no restriction to his freedom to score as many runs as he can rightfully earn. He is not forced to stop batting by the simple act of batting well.

There is an additional freedom allowed by the Laws of Cricket. As long as the ball remains in play, the runners can keep running and score as many runs as their speed and courage will allow. There is no restriction which limits the running or the scoring.

Now back to information on the boundary rope. Unlike Baseball, there are no massive walls (ivy covered or not) that control the flow of the ball. The entire playing area is encircled with a simple rope, usually only a few inches high, which marks the difference between a ball still in play and a ball that has gone for 4 or 6.

Freedom Score	Cricket	3
	Baseball	0

CHAPTER FOUR

Freedom Four

Who's on First and Where Is Silly Mid-Off?

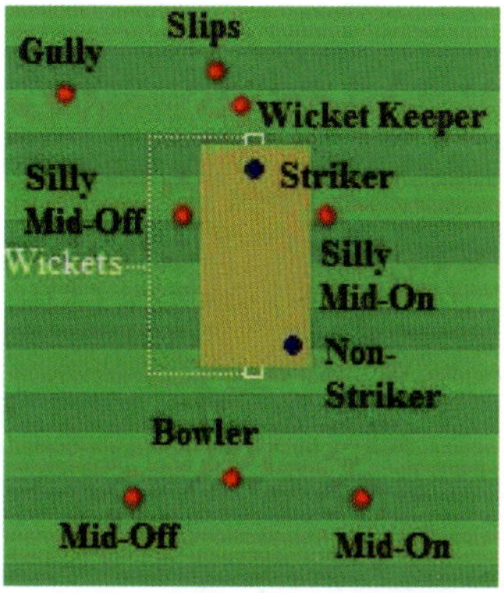

What's that you say? How can setting the fielders have any freedoms or restrictions? Well, just read on and you will begin to understand. While both games allow for fielders to be placed just about anywhere on the field of play, the freedom to do so is regularly practiced in Cricket and only rarely so in Baseball.

The freedom here is not an issue of rules or laws of the respective games, but one of the social pressure of what is commonly done and what is not.

To illustrate the point of how much pressure there is in Baseball to confirm to the restrictions of the norm, the players are usually indentified by the place where they stand on the field. A list follows below.

The Infield	**The Outfield**
1 Pitcher (Bowler in Cricket)	7 Left Field
2 Catcher (Wicketkeeper in Cricket)	8 Center Field
3 First Base	9 Right Field
4 Second Base	
6 Short Stop (sort of Second and ½ Base)	
5 Third Base	

The pressure from these norms is so pervasive and restrictive that the positions are listed by number and the scorebooks refer to the positions involved in the out and not the players' names. The numbers alongside the position listed above indicate the positional placeholder. The Short Stop position is an oddity in every way. However, I'll leave that to a Baseball book writer to explain. A scorebook entry would go like this: If a ball is hit near the second baseman and he fields it and throws it to the first baseman to get the batter run out, the scorebook would read simply 4-3. If a batter hits the ball in the air to Left Field and is caught out, the scorebook entry reads just 7. Here we are dealing not only with the restriction of the behavior, but with the stripping of individual identity. Does seem like the American way to you?

Another layer of freedom is stripped from the player by way of what equipment he allowed to use at his designated position. Baseball allows all players in the field to wear a glove/mitt. However, only the designated first baseman may where a first baseman's glove and only the designated catcher can wear the catcher's mitt.

To be fair, it should be mentioned that there are "shifts" in Baseball where the fielding team may move three players to one side of the infield and perhaps even move the outfielders more to one side than the other. These are rare occurrences and even when the players are moved, their position numbers (and glove/mitt restrictions) go with them.

Cricket

As was mentioned in an earlier chapter, there are eleven players in Cricket, nine fielders, the Bowler, and the Wicketkeeper. As was also mentioned, these eleven fielders must cover a tremendous amount of territory.

Where the players are located is dictated by the situational field management of the captain (possibly with input from the bowler or wicketkeeper) and not by fixed names, numbers, or locations. Regardless of where a Cricketer is stationed, he is never stripped of his name or identity. If a Cricket batsman hits a ball in the air and is caught out, the out is recorded giving credit to the two people responsible. Those people being the bowler and fielder who caught the ball. Using the names for the fielders: such an out would be recorded Caught Stevens, Bowled Blaney.

Now, I would truly be remiss if I didn't let the American readership in on some of the amazingly creative names for the fielding positions in Cricket. Keep in mind that these are general location areas and not specific spots. Also keep in mind, that the player retains his identity regardless of where he is standing. Most of the fielding names in Cricket are wonderful and wonderfully amusing, but I have included a few of my favorites. They are listed below.

Silly Mid-on or Silly Mid-off	Slip
Fine Leg	Gully
Short Leg	Long-on and Long-off

It is also important to point out that there are several positions in Cricket which are regularly played by more than one player at a time. As an example, it is normal to have 3 slips or 2 gullies in particular game situations. Since cricketers must cover so much ground, it is necessary to have nobody at all at certain positions depending on the game situation and the freedom of choice available when the team sets the field.

This freedom is regularly exercised when the batsman changes and can even be exercised on a ball-by-ball basis.

There is another aspect to the freedom of player placement in Cricket. Actually, this freedom extends to almost every single aspect of the game itself. The aspect of freedom is that all the decisions that are made on the field of play are made by the Captain, sometimes with consultation of teammates, and not by any non-playing team official such as a coach or manager.

Once the players cross the boundary rope, they are totally in charge of their own outcomes. There is no being oppressed by "The Man" going on in Cricket. It is the team captain, one of their very own, who makes the tough choices once the game actually begins. There is no assistance/interference from beyond the field of play, especially by a non-playing coach or manager who is still wearing a player's uniform. What's up with that?

In a very *American Frontier* sort of way, the players have to address all the problems that occur own their own. Where should the fielders be placed? Which bowler should be bowling at which time? All the strategy of the game is placed on the shoulders of the men who are actually doing the work. What could be more American than to have the players work together and figure things out all alone, out there in middle?

Freedom Score	Cricket	4
	Baseball	0

CHAPTER 5

Freedom Five

Thank You, We've Had Enough Batting

In Baseball, there are very specific rules about the process of how an inning goes and how the overall game flows. There are nine innings in a typical full game with each team batting once in each inning. Each team bats until there are three outs in their inning and then the other team bats in the same fashion.

The home team automatically goes into the field first and bats last in each inning. If the game remains tied with the scores level at the end of nine innings, there is no actual rule that ends a Baseball game.

There is one variant to this condition. If the game is permanently stopped by the umpires due to weather, it may still be considered a valid game. If that game gets past the half-way point then the game counts as being completed. The half-way point is the end of the visiting team's fifth time at bat.

Beyond the weather exception mentioned above, each team is compelled to bat for all three outs in each inning until the game is completed. There is no freedom of flexibility whatsoever when it comes which team bats first, how many outs each inning will be, or how many innings will be played.

By contrast, even these core principals of the game have significant freedom in Cricket. Let's open with who bats first. Before a Cricket match begins, there is a coin toss. The team captain that wins the toss has the freedom to choose whether his team will bat or field first. Yes, you read that correctly. The game hasn't even started yet and the Cricket captain is already able to exercise his freedom. Even on something as critical and fundamental as who will face the first ball is entirely in the hands of the captain.

Like Baseball, Cricket has a designated rhythm for the batting. While there are only two innings in Cricket (another book coming on that idea), each team is allowed to bat until they are out for that inning and then the other team bats. All players are allowed to bat in each inning. Unlike Baseball, there is no arbitrary number of outs (3) that signal the end of the allowable inning. Each team is allowed to bat until there are 10 outs. The reason that there are only 10 outs even though there are 11 players is that the players must bat in pairs and the 10th out leaves the 11th player without a batting partner so he is retired "not out" for that inning.

Now, here comes the very, very best part. The reason I kept using the phrase *allowed to bat* is that there is no Law in Cricket that requires the team to send all its players out to bat. At any point in the team's inning, the captain can simply Declare that his team is no longer batting and their inning is over. That's it, the captain has 100% freedom to decide when his team is done batting.

This is both an amazing freedom and a tremendous strategic option. If the captain decides his team has built up a large enough lead, he can surrender the rest of the outs of that inning and set about trying to get the other team out before the match ends.

Declaring is one of many fascinating aspects of Cricket strategy that keep the suspense high even across a five day match. It is also an amazingly American type of thing to do.

By declaring, and thereby surrending his team's opportunity to score any more runs in that inning, he is basically saying "Bring it!" It is a challenge that says the other team can't possibly pass his team.

Go out there, build a big lead, and the then let the other team come after you in a run chase. Declaring is a "throw down" on the other team. It conveys an essence of Big, Bold, and Invincible. What could be more American than that?

Freedom Score	Cricket	5
	Baseball	0

CHAPTER 6

The Final Freedom Score

Please Get Out Your Scorecards Boys and Girls

Now, dear reader, I will recap what we have learned in the previous Freedom chapters. I will also present a few other items of comparison for your kind consideration.

Freedom 1 Pitching/Bowling and Batting

Clearly, the rules of Baseball have rendered the actions of the pitcher and batter so rigid that it is a small miracle that anyone bothers to try at all. Perhaps this is why when the success rate of the batter is above 30%, people find this a triumphant effort.

The Cricket bowler and batsman, in stark contrast, have a massive amount of freedom which they use as methods of self expression much to the enjoyment of all.

Cricket 1 Baseball 0

Freedom 2 Where to Hit the Ball

After covering the menacing presence of the Foul Lines in Baseball, I was almost tempted to write the Baseball Commissioner and suggest the lines be chalked in as Red rather than white. Red being a color that is so much more clearly associated with menacing forces, like maybe… Communism. I'm not saying, I'm just saying.

Upon reviewing the explanation of the freedom available to a Cricket batsman, I recalled many an amazing hit (even some that were caught out) going any which way much to the delight of the attending crowd.

Add to those points the very odd Baseball idea that when a batter does his very best, he is then forced to stop batting and you begin to wonder why anyone tries at all.

Cricket 2 Baseball 0

Freedom 3 Running, or Not

As one considers the absurdity and humiliation of having a batter to try advance when he has hit the ball three feet, it makes one feel true pity for these finely tuned athletes as they make that dejected jog toward a desperately forgone conclusion.

When the comparison is made to the freedom allowed to the Cricket batsman, it hardly seems fair. Certainly, Cricketers make errors in running judgment and they can get themselves in equally hopeless situations. However, the key turning point is that it is up to the players to decide who runs and who doesn't, not the rules.

Cricket 3 Baseball 0

Freedom 4 What Are Those Guys Doing Over There?

Admittedly, Baseball has a much more organized set of position names and locations. However, is it really the American way to force a man to stay put so much so that he loses his individual identity?

Of course, the Cricket names are a bit odd and many of the positions are left empty on every ball. However, the beautiful freedom that allows the captain to place any fielder just about anywhere he wants just about whenever he likes is just too good a deal to pass up. Also, not having a non-player messing about (especially not one dressed as a player and coming onto the field of play) provides a much better setting for individual leadership and team bonding.

Cricket 4 Baseball 0

Freedom 5 That Will Be All, Thank You

When the moment is right and the captain is ready, a Cricket team can just Declare it is finished and dare the other team to catch them. No waiting around until a certain number of outs are made. No restrictions on when you can force the other team to get out there and bat. When you think you can hold a lead, you can take your chance and see if you team is strong enough to protect it.

Cricket 5 Baseball 0

Well, there is the final tally. There is no disputing the results. There need be no recount nor any run-off. The results are in. Cricket is clearly more American than Baseball.

There are many other fascinating elements to the great game of Cricket that simply wouldn't fit into the chapter format of this small book. However, some of them are so compelling that I feel honor bound to include them here. Now, a few other items for your continued reading pleasure.

1) Well Done, Sir!

One of my most favorite aspects of Cricket is what happens when a particular player does something particularly well. For instance, when a Cricket batter reaches a certain run total (say 50 runs, or a 100 runs) everyone in attendance will clap by way of congratulations. Yes, this happens even when the batsman is a member of the visiting side. Rather than booing, or throwing something at the player, everyone claps. Sadly, this is a case where Cricket is not very American. I can only wish that American fans would behave this way.

2) Stealing

In Baseball, stealing is very much encouraged. In fact, the ability to steal is highly valued and stolen bases have their own statistical category. No such concept exists in Cricket. All advancement of the runners must be come by honestly. Here again, I can only wish that the Americans would behave this way.

3) The Designated Hitter

Even among Baseball fans, this one is very troublesome. So troublesome, in fact, that Major League Baseball can't even get both Leagues to play by the same rules. In Baseball's American League, there is an allowance where a player only bats and never plays in the field. In order to not have an extra batter, this player hits instead of one of the players in the field. This non batting player is almost always the pitcher. There is nothing like this in Cricket.

4) Substitutes

Substitution is very regular part of Baseball. Any player can be replaced for any reason or no reason at all. The only restriction is that no player can re-enter the game. However, with 25 players on the active roster for any game this does go on and on. Most commonly substituted is the pitcher. In fact, it is not unusual for a team to make two or three pitching substitutes during the course of a regular game. Here again, there is no direct analog in Cricket. In Cricket, substitutes are allowed under very rare circumstances and no substitute can bowl or play wicketkeeper.

5) Replacing the Ball

Baseball umpires regularly replace the ball during the course of a game. First and foremost is the case when a ball leaves the field of play.

Whenever a ball goes beyond the fence in Baseball, a new ball is put into play. The umpire is actually allowed to switch to a new ball whenever he sees fit. This problem is so acute, that the home team must have 90 new balls ready for play before the game begins. An average game will use between 40 and 50 balls. All of this happens while each team typically pitches only about 120 total balls. In Cricket the ball is always returned into play unless the ball is just about mutilated or when The New Ball enters play after about 480 balls are bowled. Learning to bowl, hit, and field the ball as the ball's condition deteriorates is another example of the can-do and make-do attitude that infuses the game of Cricket.

6) The End of the Game

It is a bit of a fallacy that Cricket takes "forever" and Baseball does not. While a Cricket Test Match can take up to five days to complete, it often ends sooner and never lasts longer than the allotted time. Baseball, on the other hand, has no time related rule that ends the game. Certainly most games end within the standard innings and they typically last less than four hours. However, there are examples when a nine inning game goes well beyond four hours and there are also examples when the game goes well beyond the standard nine innings. It is also important to point out that Cricket has the two shorter forms of One Day (typically lasting about 9 hours), and Twenty20 (typically lasting about 3) that also have very specific endings.

SECTION THREE

Stuff that didn't fit in the first two sections

An Attempt to Explain a Few Things

America!

First and foremost, I want to explain that I truly and deeply love America. In fact, my love for America is one of the reasons I wrote this book. For too long, Americans have accepted the restricted freedoms of the game of Baseball rather than having a sporting revolution and throwing off the shackles of the game.

From my view, freedom is worth fighting for and I am happy to be the guy leading the fight. The more people I can get to start paying attention to Cricket, the more people will be able to embrace the freedom of the game. Perhaps I can pull off the sporting equivalent of Independence Day and lead America from the tyranny of Baseball and into the promised land of Cricket.

America is a great combination of immigrant cultures and practices. Embracing a truly global game like Cricket would be yet another example of how great this country really is.

Baseball

To be clear, I don't hate the game of Baseball and I don't hate the people that play or watch it. It should be obvious that I don't feel the game represents the core principals of freedom that makes this country great.

It is my continued hope for enlightenment of these troubled and confused souls that drives me to spread the good word of Cricket. It is my firm belief that the country which basically invented freedom should have a summer game that allows its players to exercise as much freedom as possible.

It is not the destruction of Baseball that I seek. Rather it is the reconnecting with America's freedom loving roots that I hope to nurture by sharing my passion for Cricket with as many Americans as possible.

Cricket

The game of Cricket is not without its flaws. Much like soccer, the international body that governs Cricket (The ICC) is much too concerned about its own political problems and about how to collect as much money as possible to pay proper attention to the game's development. There are also problems with the perennial failures of a few of the Test Nations (somewhat analogous to a world-wide Major League Baseball) with no clear path to raise the overall quality of play. On balance, the "Associate Nations" do have some opportunities to play against the big boys in the two shorter forms of the game.

Statistics

Baseball and Cricket both provide ample opportunity for scorekeeping and recordkeeping. While there are significant differences in how some of the key categories are represented, runs and batting average chief among them, both games have a special attraction to those who enjoy comparing and contrasting the stats of various players or of various eras.

Suffice it to say, if you like Baseball numbers you will love what you can keep track of in Cricket. The interest is high on both sides of the sporting equation and discussions around these numbers might just lead to a very heady discussion about the attributes of each game.

The Night Watchman

The Night Watchman is a Cricketing phenomenon so complex that it probably deserves a book of its own. It could also be a separate Freedom chapter in a book like this one. The basic idea here is another strategy element of Cricket. As the day's batting draws to a close and the light starts to become tricky, some captains don't want to send in a "quality" batsman to face the shadows and the fading light when an existing batsman gets out and a new man must be sent it.

The thinking here is that you would send in a "lower order" batsman and just have him poke and prod the ball around until it becomes too dark to bat. The general hope is that this batsman can hang around long enough to see the day through and then start fresh in the morning. The freedom is in the fact that the captain can send out anybody who is not already out to bat next regardless of the perceived batting order. In Baseball, this is against the rules and the "incorrect" batter is automatically ruled out.

Of course, the counter argument to sending in this lower order batsman is that if he possesses good enough control with the bat to handle this difficult assignment why is he not batting higher up in the order?

While I have no strong feelings one way or the other about the night watchman, I do enjoy dropping the conversational bait and then stepping back to see what happens as people defend their respective opinions.

A Confusing List of Terms

Without writing a much, much larger book and without taking all of you out to a few Cricket matches (that would be a blast!), it is simply not possible for me to actually explain everything about Cricket. The same is true for having to explain Baseball to my cricket loving readers. However, I do feel a certain obligation to at least provide some semblance of a glossary for the bravest of you to read and try to understand each other's game. The list only includes a fraction of the terms that you will encounter in either game. Just enough to get you started.

There are three parts to this list of terms. Somewhat similar words, Baseball words, and Cricket words.

Somewhat Similar Words – Format Baseball/Cricket

Batter/Batsman Both games have players that attempt to hit a thrown ball with a bat. In Baseball, the player with the bat is called the Batter. In Cricket, the players with the bat is called the Batsman. Oh yeah, in Cricket the Batsmen bat in pairs with one doing the hitting (the Striker) and one not (the Non-Striker)

Batting Average Both games use the term Batting Average and the meanings, in the purest sense, are the same. However, the calculation of the Batting Average is very different. The average of a Baseball Batter conveys how often he safely reaches at least one base due to his own hitting. In Cricket, the average conveys how many runs a Batsman accumulates before getting out.

Batting Order Both games use the term Batting Order. In Baseball, the batting order is fixed and must be followed exactly. In Cricket, the order is much more flexible.

Fielder Both games use the term Fielder to indicate a player who attempts to gather the ball and get the Batter/Batsman out.

Inning/Innings Both games use the term Inning/Innings to indicate all the batting has been completed for a team. However, a Baseball inning always contains exactly three outs (unless the home team is leading at the end of the game) for both teams. In Cricket, an innings can have any number of outs from zero to ten depending on the freedom exercised by the batting team's captain and the game situation.

Out Both games use the term Out to indicate that a player has been dismissed. Each game has myriad ways for the batter/batsman to get out.

Outfield Both games use the term Outfield to indicate the portion of the playing surface that is farthest from the Batter/Batsman

Run Both games use the term Run to indicate a score being made. However, the making of runs means something very different. In Baseball a run is scored when any player successfully moves across the first three bases and then reaches Home Plate. In Cricket a run is scored every time the two batsmen safely switch ends.

Single Both games use the term Single to indicate that the Batter/Batsman would advance by one. The advancing means something very different. In Baseball a single means that the batter advances one base and it in no way conveys that any runs have been scored. Other players may also be safely advancing. In Cricket a single means that both batsmen have safely switched ends and one run is scored.

Umpire Both games use the term Umpire to indicate one of the people who regulate play and decide Outs among other rules/Laws interpretations. In Baseball, there are four on-field Umpires for a regular season game and six for the play-offs. In Cricket, there are two on-field Umpires.

Baseball Words

Pitcher The pitcher is the Baseball player who throws the ball toward the batter. A typical Baseball game sees the pitcher replaced a few times. If the pitcher is replaced, he is retired for the rest of the game.

Catcher The catcher is the Baseball player who is positioned immediately behind the Batter. The catcher is only inches behind the batter and only inches in front of the Home Plate Umpire. The catcher typically wears a great deal of protective gear including a large specialized glove called a catcher's mitt.

Balk When a Baseball pitcher violates one of the many rules that restrict his freedom on where to stand and how to deliver the ball to the batter, a Balk is called. When this occurs, various rewards are given to the batting team including the possibility of the batting team getting a run.

Double Play and Triple Play In Baseball it is fairly regular for the fielding team to get more than one player out on a single batted ball. As the names imply, a Double Play means two outs and a Triple Play means three.

Home Run When a batter hits the ball outside the boundary fence (in Fair territory) without the ball hitting the ground, the hit is called a Home Run. All of the batting team's players who are on any base then complete the base running cycle and finish at Home Plate to have their run scored. There are variants, based on the number of runs scored, Solo Home Run, Two Run Home Run, Three Run Home Run, and Grand Slam (4 run). Four is the maximum amount of runs possible with one hit in Baseball.

Ball A pitch that the Umpire determines is not satisfactory.

Strike A pitch that the Umpire determines is satisfactory.

Pinch Hitter and Pinch Runner A player who is substituted for a batter or a runner in a particular game situation in order to enhance his team's chances at scoring runs. The player who is replaced is automatically retired for the game. The "pinch" player is often then replaced again before his team takes the field.

Bunt When a batter deliberately hits a ball a very short way and tries to catch the fielders off guard so he can advance to first base, this is called a Bunt. The strategy around this hit is far too complex to cover here. Basically, a fast player is trying to pull a fast one on the fielders rather than hit the ball in the traditional way.

Rubber A two foot long by six inch wide strip from which the pitcher must deliver the ball to the batter. The rubber is sixty feet six inches from Home Plate.

Mound A circular (18 feet in diameter) raised dirt area, which encircles the Rubber, where the pitcher stands to deliver the ball to the batter. The height of the mound where the rubber located is generally between fifteen and eighteen inches. In essence, the pitcher throws the ball "down-hill" to the batter.

Reliever/Closer A typical day's work for a Baseball pitcher is about 120 pitches. At that point, he is usually replaced by a reliever/relief pitcher. The reliever might be there for 20 or 30 pitches or he might just be there for 1. It is a very situational thing. The Closer is a special relief pitcher who enters the game when the victory decision is about to be made. Here again, he might only be in for 1 ball. The specialty here is to handle the pressure and get the last (one/few/whatever) batter(s) out to secure the victory for his team. Generally, relievers are a bit eccentric and closers are even more so.

Extra Innings If a Baseball game is tied at the end of nine full innings, the rules call for the game to go until a winner is determined. The teams continue to alternate batting (three outs per side) until the either 1) the home team gets ahead during their half of an inning or 2) the visiting team is still ahead after the home team is all out after their half of an inning. All innings beyond nine are called extra innings.

Cricket Words

Wicket The word wicket has many uses and meanings in Cricket. For the sake of simplicity, we will use the most direct meaning. The wicket is the set of three wooden stumps and the two wooden bails that are right behind the batter. It is the wicket that the batter is protecting while he bats.

No Ball If something goes wrong with the bowler's delivery, the Umpire can declare a no ball and then award one run to the batting team. The batsman, if he is quick and clever, can still try and hit the ball without any fear of getting out via the hit. There is a still a danger of being run out, if he decides to run.

Over An over represents six balls bowled. At the end of each over, a different bowler comes in and the batsmen switch places with each other.

Hat Trick If a bowler gets three batters out with three consecutive balls he has gotten a Hat Trick. Long ago, in appreciation of this feat, the bowler was given a hat. Just for the record, this term was first used in Cricket (1858) and then adopted by other sports such as ice hockey.

Follow-on If the team that bats second in the first innings is 200 or more runs behind when they are all out, the team in the lead can force the trailing team to bat again immediately. The trailing team will have to score at least enough runs to bring the score even in their second inning or they will lose the match without even making the other team bat twice.

Crease The crease is the area where the batsman typically begins play for each bowled ball. He is not required to stay there like a batter must stay in the batter's box.

Wicket Keeper This is the Cricket fielder whose position is behind the batsman. When a fast bowler is bowling, the wicket keeper is very far behind the batsman. When a spinner is bowling, the wicket keeper is much closer to the batsman. In any event, the wicket keeper has very little protective gear beyond a helmet and his gloves. It should be noted that the wicket keeper is the only Cricketer allowed to wear gloves.

All Rounder This is a term used for a cricketer that has strong talents in batting and bowling. While all bowlers must bat and some batsmen do bowl on occasion, the All Rounder does both well.

Maiden An over is considered a maiden over when the batsman doesn't score. You in the back, stop that snickering! The over is a considered a wicket maiden if there is no scoring and a wicket is taken.

Ton/Century When a batsman scores at least 100 runs in the same inning, he is said to have reached a Ton/Century. 200 is a double Century, etc.

Drinks/Lunch/Tea These are the names of certain planned stoppages of play during a Cricket match. The purpose of the breaks should be self-evident. Keep in mind that Test Cricket is played for many hours each day and for as long as five days. Therefore, some enforced and regular breaks are both welcome and necessary.

Stumps This term, primarily used in Australia, signifies the end of play for the day. When the Umpire has called for play to stop, he removes the bails from atop the stumps and then everyone goes for a drink. Lovely.

Googly A googly is a bowled ball that "breaks" the opposite way that it should. In other words, rather than moving away from the batsman's legs and toward the "off side", the googly spins the other way from the "off side" toward the batsman's legs.

A Bit about the Author

Michael Johnson lives with his lovely bride Kathryn in a yurt among the peaks of Nepal. Oh, no wait, that's a different story entirely.

Michael Johnson is best known as the fastest man in the World as he is the only man in history to win the 200m and 400m sprint events in the same Olympics. Oh, no wait, that is a different Michael Johnson.

Steady on.

Ok, here is the real deal.

Michael Johnson does live with his lovely bride Kathryn. However, it is in a quiet house on a nice patch of God's green earth in Wisconsin. Which is, by the way, in AMERICA!

Michael is the proud father of three sons who also live in Wisconsin and are up to all sorts of interesting things. He is also the proud father-in-law of Whitney.

In case this book has not made the point clear enough, Michael is a complete cricket nutter. He has seen professional cricket in four different countries on three different continents and amateur cricket in a few more. He is always in search of his next opportunity to watch cricket or, at the very least, talk about it.

Michael is also the USA Ambassador to the Don Bradman Museum in Bowral, New South Wales, Australia.

When not busy with his family, the cricket, or running his strategic consulting firm, Full Potential Associates, Michael is usually writing another oddly interesting book.

Cricket Pictures from around the World

A Few Pictures from America

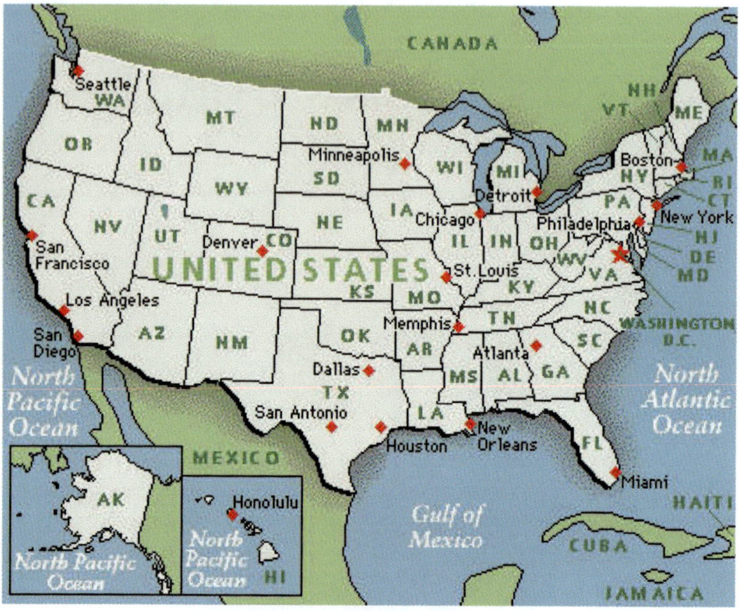

The sign for Cope Field at Haverford College, Haverford Pennsylvania.

The "Founding Sign" at Merion Cricket Club, a few minutes from Haverford.

The author with a Don Bradman bat. The stance needs work!

A Few Pictures from Australia

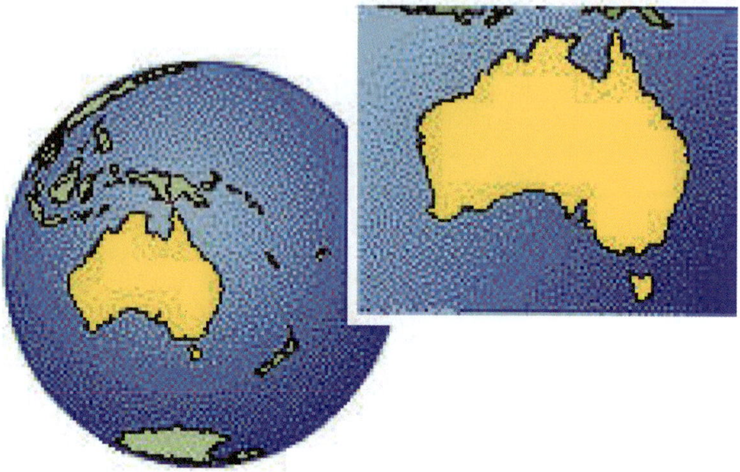

Michael Johnson with a statue of Sir Donald Bradman taken at the Bradman Museum in Bowral, New South Wales.

Members' Entrance at the Sydney Cricket Ground.

Michael Ball and Michael Johnson and some award winning cattle.

The Boundary rope at the Bradman Oval.

Pictures from England

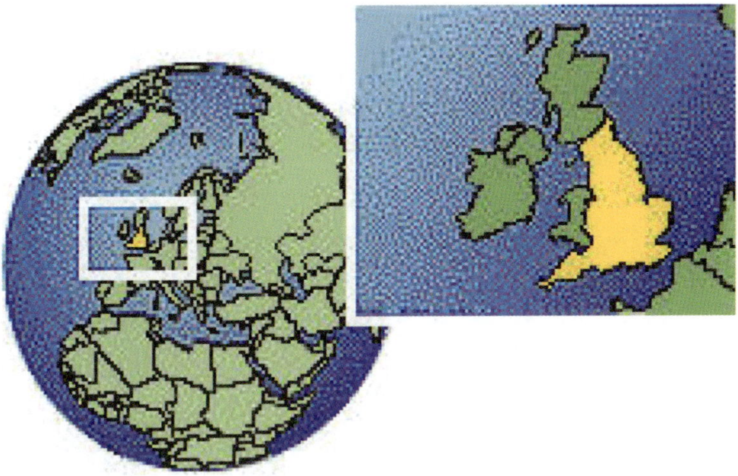

The Victorian era Members Pavilion at Lord's in London complete with a nice view of the famous Long Room.

The Boundary rope at Lord's. As you can see, it really is a rope.

Pictures from the Caribbean

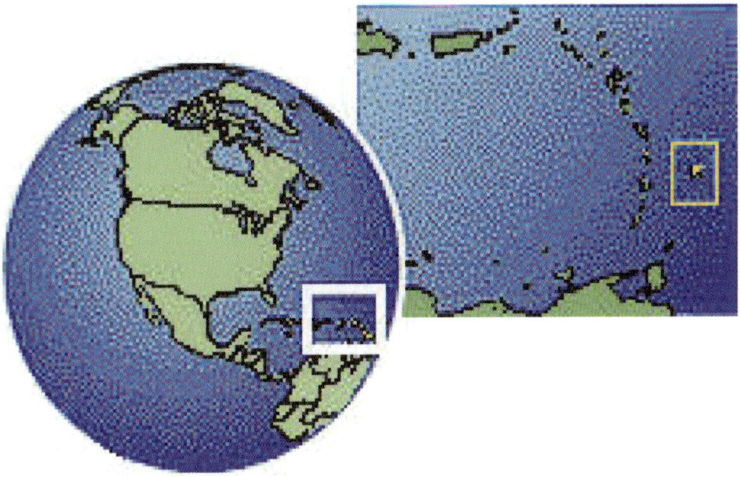

Michael Johnson with Steve Harmison on that amazing night in Barbados.

Frank Coster in front of a statue of Sir Garfield (Gary) Sobers. Kensington Oval, Barbados.

The Garfield Sobers Pavilion. Kensington Oval, Barbados.

The Beginning

Now there may be some of you in the global reading audience who may be confused by the placement of this chapter. A lot of people have told me the "The Beginning" chapter should be, well, um, at the beginning!

While the chapter comes at the end of this book, it is my hope that it will represent the beginning of something special. Ideally, an expanded understanding and enjoyment of cricket by millions of Americans and a dialog about the great game between you and me.

If anything I have written in this book has in any way made you curious or interested in cricket, then I hope you put in a little effort to try and find a local game and watch it. As I mentioned, there are hundreds of teams playing all over the country. You can visit the USACA website at http://usaca.org/to find out the team closest to you.

If you have any questions or comments, please send them to me via The Takoma Ridge Media website http://takomaridgemedia.com/.Being able to interact with you will make me a better advocate for cricket and should lead to even better publications in the future. I wrote this book because I love Cricket and because I love America. If I can bring these two loves closer together, I will consider this effort a ringing success.

All the sentiment is the same for my international readers. If you regularly go to the cricket, go more often. If you don't go regularly, then start! Please also jump in on the website and send in your questions and comments.

I have no doubt that the world would be a better place if more people were playing, watching, and talking about cricket.

Thanks for the reading the book and please do keeping the conversation going!

Michael's sponsorship brick at the International Cricket Hall of Fame
Bowral, New South Wales, Australia

6311662R00044

Printed in Great Britain
by Amazon.co.uk, Ltd.,
Marston Gate.